WHY THE HELL I CAN'T STUDY

NO NONSENSE, ONLY PROVEN METHODS

JD

Copyright © Jd
All Rights Reserved.

ISBN 979-888606029-4

Touching the feet of my Guru Paramahansa Yogananda,

Namskaram to lord almighty, Bhagwan Shri Jambheshwar, Lord Saibaba, and my parents.

I Dedicate this book to my wife Krati, my sister Poonam and my son Vivan.

Contents

Contents

Spcial Thanks

I want to thank some amazing people without their help It would have been impossible to write and share these experiences with my readers. I am extremely thankful to Mr. Amitoj Singh, My student Karishma, and Mr.Abhishek for their endless effort during this project.

CHAPTER ONE

Some Questions

Before you even start reading the first page of this book, let me ask you a question. You can give its answer in any manner you like except one

And that is **"I don't know "**

The question is **"why do you think that you can't be a national topper"?**

Woohh ! A big and tough question,

If you are already not a national topper chances are there that your mind will go blank.

Let me ask one more time and please try to find some answers this time. "What is holding you back? I mean a national topper is also a human being; he/she has the same body structure and mind as you. If he/she can be, then why not you? What is the difference "?

So again **"why do you think that you can't be a national topper"?**

When I came across this question for the very first time, my mind went blank. I really couldn't think of anything. And when the questioner asked again, some of my answers were as follows and I am sure most of you have got some answers

1. I don't know (the typical).

2. I don't have that sharp mind.

3. I don't have that much good memory.

4. I hardly can score 3rd-4th position in my class, how I can be a national topper?

5. I don't know how they study? I mean, I spend the same amount of time as they do but the results are still disparate.

6. They are kind of born intelligent.

Now let's examine these answers a bit.

1. **Sharp mind:** how do you know, apart from their scores? How can you surely say that they have a sharp mind? Do you have any measuring devices?

2. **Good memory:** let's say someone is a topper in the science stream. And he/she started to read a book about accountancy. So, do you really think that they can recall the whole book just after 1st reading? I think you know the answer.

3. **Born intelligent: Yes,** some of them are. But we all know, even by scientific facts that it is not the case for every successful person on this planet.

And rest all three answers are indicating that YOU DONT KNOW. So, what exactly are you looking for?

Their study methods? The very source of their brainpower? Their ability to understand? Their ability to memorize? Their ability to solve the tough questions?

Alternatively, the fact that

HOW YOU CAN GET THOSE ABILITIES?

I think the last line will do enough job for you. And by the end of this book, I will give you an answer to this very question. And not only this but I will also discuss various scientifically proven methods which will help you to get these abilities within a specific time limit.

CHAPTER TWO

Why Me

However, before that let me first tell you why you should listen to me

In the early days of my student life, I was quite a studious person. Although, not good with grades because I was so egoistic and careless that I never took the exams very seriously, but yeah! I was a bookworm. Once I knew all the answers to the exam, still, I left some of them because I got bored. Not only I could study but also, I liked to study very much. I was able to understand almost every book of my standard or even some books that were beyond my standard without the help of any external resource. At that time, I used to think "why do other students hate studying so much, and why they are afraid of exams so much?"

For me it was kind of, taking a bath. Just go in, turn on the shower and enjoy. I never experienced the fear of exams or the fear of failure. Time passed, my priorities changed. I thought being studious is a boring lifestyle. I wanted to be that guy who knows how to fight and how to impress girls and I was sure that the backbenchers were more qualified than class toppers when it comes to impressing a girl also that guy is always considered the coolest guy in the school or college.

So, in my college life, I left my studious image behind and joined the backbencher's club. I did everything, except study and drugs.

And then a time came when the tables turned, Now I wasn't able to understand how someone can study for hours. My mindset had completely changed. I was not that old studious and obedient guy anymore. None of my college mates could imagine that I can study for half an hour straight (not in a day but in months). And it was not only them, I too was not in a state to imagine myself seeing study, so bringing things to action was beyond my capability. I persuaded backbencher's lifestyle so hard that within a few months my will to study, my methods, and my focus all were lost from the deepest corners of my mind.

To give you a simple idea about how bad I was in the study, let me give you some examples of my study pattern of that time.

1. I wasn't able to understand even a single line of the first paragraph of any book.

2. My friends used to help me by telling me in simple language what was written in the book.

3. I was not able to study for more than 5 minutes in a single sitting (before college I used to study for 12-14 hours straight)

4. I was drunk with daydreaming almost 24 hours a day.

When I chose to be a backbencher, I was sure that I could leave that lifestyle any time I wanted to. I thought the transition would be effortless as I already was a studious person once. But believe me, once I got trapped, it was one of the most difficult issues ever faced by me. Although with lots of struggle, I finally succeeded.

And during this **studious to failure to again studious** journey I got some amazing insights which not only helped me to get back on track also with the help of these techniques, I helped hundreds of students to achieve their aim.

CHAPTER THREE

Real Problems

After college, I chose to be a Physics faculty for JEE (Joint Entrance Examination). One of the toughest exams in India. So, I had to study for this because the students I was going to face were to be some of the brightest minds in India. To keep them satisfied, I had to study again. So, I made up my mind and bought the tasks to be done in action. I tried to study, but again the newly acquired habits made it complicated. For some time being, I studied just enough to stop students from questioning my knowledge.

Over time I met newer students, parents, and even teachers every year. I came to know their problems. I saw the very drastic difference between the actual problem faced by the student and the parents or teacher version of the student's problem.

For example, most parents think that their child spends a lot of time over the phone and he/she is not interested in studies. That is not true. As far as I know, most of the students who choose paths for competitive exams really want to improve their ranks, study hours. They really will be thrilled if they could solve the toughest problems of the books. But the actual problem is that when they try to do so, most of them can't even understand the language of the question. Even if they do, after that they don't know how to approach. In fact, most of them wonder "what the first line should I write" forget the whole and correct solution. Some of them make petty mistakes despite knowing everything; they always get the wrong answer. These small basic problems slowly break their will and focus and after 100 daily defeats, a student (even a very motivated, inspired, and well intentional student) puts down his/her weapons and admits permanent defeat.

And then comes the CELL PHONE and social media.

Parents and teachers saw only the "Cell phone and Social Media" part. That is the biggest problem. Because a student not only got trapped in a problem, also his/her mentor doesn't know the root cause of the problem.

As a full forced backbencher, I knew these problems from the very core of my heart, and over time I got to know the teacher's version (initially, as a fresher and later on, as an experienced teacher) of how should someone study and how a person can change his study methods and improve his grades.

There are many people from whom a student can get advice regularly about how to improve their grades or how to score a good rank in competition (like teachers, parents, and even motivational speakers). The problem with their advice is that they present only the topper's version of life. They can only talk about how good your life will be if your grades improve, or if you secure a good rank in any professional examination. But they have no idea or maybe never speak about the problems faced by the average students. They couldn't understand that most of the students wants to study but couldn't do it and most of the mentors don't realize this factor.

They thought that a student didn't want to do it. So, they failed to understand that there is a huge gap between wanting and doing.

When an average student becomes a bit aware of his poor situation, he tries to study more. Although in this journey, there are lots of obstacles. Most of the time, teachers or parents consider these obstacles more like a stupid excuse made by a student or they don't consider them as a big issue. But for a student, these are real issues. Some of these reasons are listed below.

· Sometimes when I try to study, I can't even understand what the writer wants to say.

· After five minutes, I feel like I have been sitting there for centuries.

· When I see unfinished syllabus or backlogs, it makes me thirsty. I feel like I should run away from the study table.

· Every day I make a timetable but never be able to follow it.

· When I solve a question, I can't even understand what is asked in the question.

· Even if I can understand the question, I don't know what should I write in the first line.

· I try to memorize the formulas and concepts but still I forget them.

· I always think that I will start fresh from next year, but after 10 days I am that same old procrastinating looser.

· I try every day and I get defeated every day.

· Even though I am trying everything and working hard, still my rank or grades are not improving.

· I think if I will give more time to study, I will lose my fun life.

· Distracted by phone.

· Maintaining a cool image in the group.

· You have to show your friend circle that you don't take your teacher very seriously, otherwise they will think less of you.

· I want to study, but that is very hard. So I try some other things like making fun of the teacher in front of my friends. In this way, at least I will not look like a complete loser and I can be one of those guys who is cool.

❧❧❧

So, when I became a teacher, my whole focus was on the average students. I wanted to discover some sort of magic wand that can transform these so-called average students into geniuses. But no matter what I tried, say motivation, tricks, reward, punishment, storytelling I didn't succeed. For 3 years I was in a state of awe, I was desperately searching for some sort of spell. But there were none.

CHAPTER FOUR

The first string of solution

Luckily, I had some very bad days in my life and because of that, I had to dwell in the area of psychology. To my surprise, I found most of the answers there,

So I started to dive **deep into human psychology, about how human brains work, how habits develop**. With my good experience of **successful – failure** student to a very keen teacher experience, it didn't take me much time to connect all the missing dots. It was all about science and human psychology. There was nothing new but there was a lot that I was not aware of (and there is a difference between not knowing and not being aware of). Then I studied myself as an object. I honestly looked deeply into every excuse which I made. And finally, I was able to define both states of mine. A studious one and a backbencher one.

Now equipped with scientific facts and experience of two different personalities along with experience as a teacher, I laid the foundation of practical motivation and technique for students. I designed a workshop for those students who are motivated but still score good marks were

beyond their reach.

I tried them upon more than 2000 students and found them very effective. Also, we started an online workshop for students where we can check the daily progress of students, the result was astonishing and even beyond my expectation. That is why I decided to write a book about this. I will try to provide you with almost the same experience as our workshops.

But first, let me tell you what the basics of these techniques are. In that way, you will be able to see how this whole smart study saga is a series of scientific methods. Not only this, the knowledge of how to do smart work will open some new dimensions of your life, If followed properly they will surely lead you towards a very successful life on many fronts.

The only condition is "you have to follow them ". just learning will not do any good. As I already said, there is a big difference between knowing something and being aware of that thing. If you are reading just for knowledge, my advice is to close this book right now and spend your precious time someplace else.

CHAPTER FIVE

Mind is our pet dog

An interesting fact about our mind is that it is just like a dog of a very powerful breed. A well-trained dog is a most loyal friend. Even in life-death situations, it will not leave our side. So, a trained mind will serve us as a most loyal servant, very protective. It will be fearless in even the harshest life situations. It will think and create some way or other even worst-case scenarios. On the other hand, an untrained dog can be very dangerous and destructive. The same is the case for the mind. An untrained mind can wreak havoc in our life. it can make us so unfocused and can fill our hearts with thousands of temptations. For example, It can make us believe (temporarily but continuously) that scrolling down on a social media page is more important than our real goals.

Let's talk some science!

Though, the science of the brain is very complex terrain. But the good thing is that we don't need to explore all of that.

Let me tell some interesting facts about brain hormones.

Dopamine makes you repeat some action, even it is totally useless. This is the hormone that is responsible for addiction. When you do something, which feels good for the first time (say social media or watching a web series). Our brain releases dopamine. It feels so good (at least to our subconscious mind) that we crave it again and again. But the problem is when we repeat our action, our body releases a less amount of dopamine with every repetition but our subconscious mind craves it more and more. So, we want to repeat that action again and again in a hope that our body will release some more of it. But here is the paradox, as we repeat our actions again and again our body releases less and less. Which leaves us overall with a dopamine thrust.

It explains that we can spend hours scrolling the social media pages, even there are really important pending works.

The second is Adrenaline, in some manner it is amazing.

Here I am giving you only two out of hundreds (maybe thousands which went unreported) examples of what this thing can do

• In 2013, in Oregon, teenage sisters Hannah (age 16) and Haylee (age 14) lifted a tractor to save their father pinned underneath.

• In 2013, in Salvage, Newfoundland and Labrador, Cecil Stuckless, a 72-year-old man lifted a Jeep to save his son-in-law pinned underneath

So, what happened here, and how this is related to our topic?

CHAPTER SIX

Minutes of Evolution

As we all know that we were just like animals not long before. It might seem long (around 2-3 million years but in the eye of evolution it is just like 24 hours.

There are lots of things which haven't changed yet.

In the animal world when an animal faces a life-death situation, some hormone is released into its body. These hormones make it either to run away from the scene (Sometimes mother deer runs for her life when a potential predator like lion or tiger is on the hunt, abandoning her calf) or to fight with their full potential (we have seen this on many social media where a dog or buffalo is confronting a lion)

So after around 2-3 million years, we are human now, but still, we have the same fight and flight mode in us. We too act in the same manner as an animal does when we face life-death situations. Sometimes this can make us really cowardly (when people leave their kids or relatives behind in warlike situations to protect their own life, though not intentionally) or can bring Superman out of us.

And the trick is, when our mind sees an uncomfortable situation, it freaks out and releases those hormones. In our daily life, most of the situations are not that dangerous, but still, our unchecked thought (thoughts like "what will happen if I fail "even though you are not failed yet) give our minds the same kind of signals that we are in great danger.

Now, what happened after releasing these hormones. the first thing is that our reflex takes charge (if they don't, it would be very difficult to survive in wild. Because if you are thinking but not acting while facing a lion you might end up in its stomach") But right now, we are neither in the wild nor our daily life situation demands some physical fight. So it makes us uneasy, worried, nervous, and hence unfocused.

So, these techniques are based on three things:

1. To break the cycle of unnecessary red signals to the mind and change it with the cycle of productive and fruitful habits.

2. To train our mind to differentiate between actual and mind-made false danger.

Because not knowing the answer to the question in the exam or what will happen to my career is not a life-death situation. you can get out of these situations. You might think that it is not possible, but believe me, if you follow these techniques, you will see a drastic change in your life.

3. For third, let's assume that your parents and you shifted to a new location because of your parent's job. Now it is day one and because of some unknown reason (just pick any) you have to go to a store which is 4 km away from your house by your cycle. People in this town are very reserved and don't like to be bothered. So, you asked your father about the location and decided not to bother any stranger

for help. As soon as you left the house your parents left the house for some work and they promised that they will return before your return. So far so good. You are cycling and enjoying the weather. And after half a kilometer you forgot the exact location, you searched your pocket for your phone for Google Maps. But, Oh! Snap, you don't have it. Now as there is nobody at home and you don't have a key so you decided to continue your journey as you have a vague idea of location.

But there are so many turns and streets. even if you will be able to reach the exact location, you will surely face lots of trouble while coming back to your house. So, what will you do? (Now you are on your own and don't want to wait in front of your house for your parents)

I bet you will apply some common sense. At every turn, you will stop for a minute and memorize where exactly you are going. You might mark some shops or buildings so that they will help you during your return. As simple as that.

Now think about this, don't you always dwell in an unfamiliar terrain when you learn something new. Everything that you want to remember is new. And most of the time you got once or twice visiting there (covering 1-2 times of the whole syllabus). Then why don't you stop at every confusing turn and just mark something which will help you to retract that information back from your brain during your exam or test?

When you are going to the vaguely known location, most of the time you can ask for help and can go there, In the same manner when you are learning or reading something 1st or 2nd time it is easy to understand those things with the help of your teacher. But when you are coming back without any help it would be very difficult to know where did you exactly come from. In the same manner, it is easy to take the information into your mind but very hard to retract during exams.

The reason is that you hadn't marked anything or didn't emphasize the confusing links, so you will feel like "was there a positive sign there or negative? Was it 3 May 1986 or 13 May 1987? Because both look very similar?

How the hell does your mind know the difference between which date was more important than any other date?

To solve this problem most students apply only one method: Revision. Now again think, if you are in a new city, then remembering a new location will take at least 3-4 days (I am talking about just one). So how are you going to remember thousands of formulas or concepts or dates in 1-To 2 revisions?

And the answer is "to stop, mark some building and emphasize the difference between two similar-looking paths"

CHAPTER SEVEN

Expections

So what you can expect from these techniques

Our mind is our dog and we can train a dog

In the same manner, you can easily train your mind by using these scientific techniques. You can boost your efficiency, your focus, and your grades. Not superhumanly but in a way better than listening to some hollow motivational lecture.

Along with, these techniques, I found that there are lots of myths in society about how to improve your grades or rank. These are very common. **Some of them are very attractive and politically correct.** But believe me, they can be very dangerous for a student who is willing to change his life but acts according to these myths.

CHAPTER EIGHT

Some Popular Myths

Let's first bust some common myths about studies that are floating in our society. Then we will go to some new and scientific methods of smart study.

No matter how big a loser you are, if you follow these methods correctly you are going to see a change not even in grades but in some other aspects of your life as well.

I don't want you to believe some sort of philosophy of mine. I myself never did. I always prefer proof and scientific facts rather than hollow and cheesy motivation. That's why I will talk about scientific techniques only. No cheesy motivation, no-nonsense.

Myths

1. Over the last 25 years (as a student as well as a teacher) I have heard parents and teachers emphasizing motivation. "Students need motivation for study" is like a motto for teachers. But believe me, on the students' side they are going to interpret it like this

"I like it when I hear stories of successful people, I want to be like them. It wants to make my mark on the world

(Well, who doesn't), and also so-called motivation makes me think this way as well".

But the problem with motivation is that it goes off within hours, sometimes within 20 -30 minutes. A student can feel thrilled and be able to turn the world upside down with his willpower because of some seminar or teacher's speech in the class yet most of the time he/she loses it just after the bell. As the routine kicks in, the motivation just says goodbye. The next day he is just the same guy with half-solved problems, unread books, and backlog syllabus.

2. **Smart study:** it's a modern and very fancy world. Everyone knows the name i.e., so-called "THE SMART STUDY". Everyone suggests it but how it should be done? Most people don't even have the slightest idea about this. Forget about students, even the smart parents and teachers don't have any concrete idea about this.

3.**There are some common Indian phrases.** In India, for motivation, or I should say emotional blackmail few sentences are very popular among parents and teachers. For example

· Your parents are doing so much for you, can't you see.

· You should study so that your parents can feel proud.

· When we were of your age, we had no A.C., coolers or car, etc. We had just a fan for the whole family. (Well when your parents were of your age, they might have not any slippers or even food, forget about fan)

. When you reach our age, you will learn how hard it is to make money.

· Study hard, otherwise you will end up just like us.

If you are a parent and feel offended by these lines, I am so sorry to hurt your feelings. But this is the truth. Even a basic book about psychology can verify that emotional blackmail weakens the personality and will of a kid. **(Also what can we expect from the truth except for its bitter taste and good results?)**

And if you are a student then it might be a case that you are jumping with joy just by reading these lines.

As I have given you a full pack of ammunition and counterarguments. But chances are that you will be doing the same when you will be of your parents' age. And the game is not about winning the argument with your parents, it's all about helping yourself and being a better version of yourself.

Being a parent is always a tough job. In some cases, it is true that parents sacrifice their wishes just to provide a good study environment for their children. But let me tell you a very honest and politically incorrect fact:

None of the above sentences can change your child's study pattern. Even, it can induce a feeling of guilt which will lead to even more destructive behavior of your child. Also, there are well-studied cases about the broken marriage and spoiled career choices of those children who were emotionally blackmailed in their childhood.

So, whether you like it or not, you must stop this kind of behavior as a parent or teacher.

4.The more hours you study, the more you get good grades.

Look! for good grades you must sit for a few hours and during these hours you should study seriously. But the vice-versa is not true. I mean if you are studying for more hours on daily basis, that doesn't give any guarantee about your grades. The key here is to devote a few hours to the required subjects with proper planning. If you don't have a proper plan, the odds are that you will get the same result which you got last year. Like they say "If You Want to Get Something Different, You Have to Do Things Differently "

Caution: I am not saying that several hours of study doesn't matter, they do but only when you have a proper plan.

5.I have lots of unclear doubts, so I won't be able to catch up with the stuff that requires a good amount of hard work: this is a myth held by most of the students. Because of poor study methods they usually don't remember the concepts which were studied in the previous standards and when these basic concepts are required later on, most of the student loses their confidence.

Believe me, you indeed need to remember your basic concepts all the time but even if you have already forgotten them then it will take just 1-2 days to memorize them again. Again! The key here is proper planning.

6. I have very poor memory: most of the average students think that for good memory, one should be god gifted. This is true for some people (who want to memorize the phone numbers of 500 people in one sitting). But for ordinary people having a good memory depends upon self-confidence and their study methods. I will talk more about this, later, in the other part of the book.

7. Toppers are not cool guys: it's just another myth held by most of the students. Being a cool guy has nothing to do with being studious. And it's true for both sides. If you are a topper, it will not give a guarantee of being cool but it's also not true that you can't be cool or be that popular guy and topper at the same time.

CHAPTER NINE

Let's start

So, we will study a common day of an average student and learn about the solutions to basic problems encountered by that student on a daily basis. Then we will talk about some basic things which are required to be a good scorer, like time table, study plan, memorizing methods and how to develop these qualities.

CHAPTER TEN

The Art of controlling your thoughts during class

For most of the students @ 9:45 A.M.-: the distance between them and the teacher is 308.05 million km

308.05 million kilometers, this is the distance between Earth and Mars.

Let's say a student enters a class at 9:30 AM and just after 10-15 minutes, the teacher who is teaching about accounts, say something like this, "you have one million in bank and interest rate is 5%"

An average student's thoughts will start to elevate like this

"One million? Oh yeah!! that's a big amount. How amazing it would be if I were a millionaire. Or wait! a billionaire. That would be much more amazing. The world would look up to me as a leader like Elon Musk who by the way, wants to send a spaceship on Mars. Wow ! how beautiful his girlfriend is. I wish my girlfriend was that beautiful, Oh wait, I wish I had a girlfriend. How cool life would be after that."

So, the teacher is in a bank and the student is on Mars. Either the teacher has to go on mars to teach or the student has to come back to earth to study more accurately in the class.

❧❧❧

This is the first and very common problem encountered by most of the students. They can't focus on what the teacher is saying just for 10 minutes straight. Even in these 10 minutes, they will either be going to mars or they will be thinking about their friends, social media messages, yesterday's small talks, or future planning.

Without being conscious about the present they won't be able to get the very first draft of the concept that the teacher is going to draw in front of them.

❧❧❧

Some of the main reasons and their solutions for this problem are:

1. Comfort zone: Imagine you are in the principal's office. Can you go to Mars while receiving a threat about getting detained? Well, honestly you can't unless you are a heavy careless daydreamer. Your mind only wonders when you are relaxed and in your comfort zone. This is what happens in the classroom also. Students usually sit with the same people and on the same seats every day, and most of the average students sit in a way so that teacher doesn't have direct sight upon them. Boom! this way a great comfort zone is created either consciously or unconsciously and the next thing you know is that you are on Mars.

So, if you are struggling with your grades and how to improve them, then I am serious when I say this, that you have to sit with new people for a change, try to sit on a new spot in the class every day. It would be better if you can sit in two front rows. You will get the proper audio, as well as your mind, will remain focused.

2. Try to set small goals. I know it's very easy to write and read about this problem. But it takes tremendous courage and self-awareness to keep yourself alert all the time. Even if you are trying very hard to do so, you will feel tired after some time (maybe within half an hour). And that's ok. It's just human nature, it's just the way we change ourselves. It's hard but you should keep doing this. And for that, you should try for 5-10 minutes first in a one-hour long lecture (if your focus is really bad). Give yourself credit (eat a candy) if you be able to stay focused for 5-10 minutes. And stop after that, start again in the next lecture at the same time, and so on. For the next day try 13 to 15 minutes.

Just be patient and within 10-15 days you will get the most out of it.

3. Lack of physical exercise: it seems obvious and most people have already heard about this and they think of it as a long-term goal or healthy lifestyle but I don't wanna start on that topic. Just start running for half an hour daily for the next 1 month and you will see how this simple trick can make you a man of great focus.

4. Healthy food: Again! I am not talking healthy lifestyle but healthy food habits reduce anxiety and help to maintain a calm mind which directly enhances your focus.

Warning: once you started don't break the chain, either don't start it or just do it amazingly.

CHAPTER ELEVEN

The Art of taking Notes

Now the teacher is teaching you and you have to take notes. Notes are a very important gadget when it comes to revision because at that time the teacher will not be there. Only these notes are going to be there. Great notes means that you will remember not only what you have written but also how you have written.

Most of the average students don't know how to take notes. They either write everything that is coming out of the teacher's mouth or just write to give themselves a sense of studying. And both ways are of no use.

So, if you want to take 100% advantage of notes, the main thing you have to understand is that it's you who is going to read them again so you have to write accordingly. And because that person is YOU. So write in a manner which is most understandable for you.

Be creative and courageous.

And for being that I mean to write in short sentences, local languages, slang, pictures, drawings, cartoons, expressions, smiles, writing with more than one or two color pens, highlighting.

One of my students used to write very offensive slang when he wants to emphasize very confusing sentences. It might not be morally correct but I am sure it gave his mind an interesting way to remember things.

Relate your confusing formulas with the most disgusting words and you will never forget them. It is all about emotions. Your mind won't remember a simple chat with people but if this chat involves something offensive about you, I am pretty sure that you will remember it even after years. Go and use that strategy in your notes.

Your notes must be like "you can love them; you can hate them but you can't ignore them"

Note down the essence, leave the obvious. Don't get afraid that you will forget everything, be confident and leave the obvious things.

Note * always make short notes as well. These are the notes of your class notes. You should make them after the second revision and always make them from your class notes (not from any textbook) and they must not be more than 10% of your class notes. You can download short notes templets from our website **www.thinkcepts.com**

These will come in handy in fast revisions and they will take your confidence to the next level.

CHAPTER TWELVE

The art of Reading

Now you are at your home and it's time for you to self-study. You declutter your study table and get yourself ready to change the world. You put your water bottle near you, put your phone on silent mode (at least for a few minutes) and open the book.

Let the magic begins,

When you start reading, you know the meaning of every individual word written there and by meaning, I mean its literal meaning. But somehow you can't comprehend what the author wants to say.

It's like the book is written in some ancient language. You are going through the same line, again and again, reading repeatedly but still not able to understand the essence.

For some students, this is a serious concern. They just with open book in thier lap, looking at it for long hours, and then they decide to take a break and after a few minutes, they try again but fail. Then again and again.

If a student continue studying this way, chances are that he/she will be get distracted either by daydreaming or social media messages, phone calls, or any impulsive act which satisfies instant gratification. Because nothing is happening on the study front. So, the mind needs something where it can get results, whether superficially.

Symptoms for this to happen: You know the language but can't understand more than two lines of a book in one sitting.

Cause: Again, the main culprit here is a lack of focus . Not like when you are in class but here your thoughts are running wild, and your eyes move way faster than your grabbing power. It's like there is no friction, nothing can stop your eyes, which slides over the sentences. Your eyes are reading so fast that your mind doesn't get enough time to comprehend what is coming through the way.

Solution: Firstly, let's think of a scenario, you are at a nice party and somehow you get into a heated debate with someone. Suddenly, that person made a very nasty comment to you. You feel a sudden rage of anger to teach him a lesson. Now in your mind, you want to kick him but most of the time we don't let such thoughts turn into actions (until it is a life-threatening case). The takeaway is that we can control our physical actions way better than our mind's actions. As we never practiced controlling our thoughts so it's quite hard for us. But the same is not the case for controlling physical action.

In the same manner, it is very hard to control the thought while studying but if we add some kind of physical activity to it, things will become very simple.

All you have to do is take a pen or a pencil and move it slowly over the line which you are reading. Read only the part where the pencil is. As you can easily control the motion of the pencil, so in this way, you will be able to control the motion of your eyes.

Initially, move the pencil very slowly so that your brain gets enough time to take the data in. You will see a tremendous result about your comprehensive power.

Secondly, some students are very restless. When they sit for studying, they see a mountain of the unfinished syllabus. They count the pages first to check how much is left to study and believe me some students count pages after every 2 minutes just to ensure that some work is done. Even reading 3-4 lines can be a very hideous task for them. They feel like they are studying for centuries and that can happen even after reading just 2-3 lines.

If you are one of those kinds, please lower your bar; lower your daily goal, for now at least.

For such students, I am telling you a very powerful and kind of like a magic trick. But the problem with this trick is that it seems hypothetical and utterly ridiculous and believe me it won't work if you just read it.

Even if you don't believe it, I highly recommend you to try it 3 times at least. It won't take more than 5 minutes.

So! Here the trick is something like that: - the next time when you sit for study, say these lines to your mind

"I know you are afraid; I know you think that so much is left to be done. I know you are afraid that you have to finish this all on time and a little time has left. But today can you please leave that aside and read-only these 2 lines for me (you can say a paragraph or 5 lines, as per your condition but the target must be very easily approachable). Only 2 lines, if you feel uncomfortable after that I will not study. I am giving you only 2 lines. After that, it's your choice "

Just say this to your mind.

Chances are there that not only your mind will stay focused on these two lines but also it will be ready to read the next 2 lines.

But you have to be quite honest with your mind all the time. You have to stop after 2 lines and have to take permission of your mind again for the next 2 lines or 4 lines.

Try it for a week and slowly you will see that the 2 lines limit is increasing from 10 lines to one page to 5 pages in a sitting and eventually you will reach your ideal goal.

Take care of your mind as you take care of a one year-old kid. Don't leave it on its own. It can't survive without your supervision and also can be very destructive if left alone.

The Art of not loosing Focus

25 minutes game

Until and unless you are not a pro or an Olympiad winner kind of person, don't study for more than 25 minutes in one sitting. There is a lot of research that proves that the human mind can be very active in learning within a short interval of 25 minutes. So even if you have amazing concentration, please don't stretch it more than 25 minutes per sitting. It will help your mind to focus in the long term.

You need to take a break for 5 minutes after every 25 minutes. You can listen to music or go for a walk during this short break.

Chances are that you already know this, as this is a very common fact. The problem with this is that students have a mind which is two-way folded.

First, if they are doing well, they don't want to leave after 25 minutes. Like if they are running for 25 minutes then they think they can run for another 25 minutes. That might be possible with studies as well but after the next 25 minutes, you are going to need a long break that might stretch to half an hour or more. So, in the long term, it will reduce your productivity.

Second, students go for a 5 minutes break but can't pull themselves back to study after this short break. Their 5 minutes break can get converted into a 3-hours movie or 1-hour call with their best friend.

So, it's better to keep a check on this kind of pitfall first. If you have a habit of long phone calls or web series, then stay away from your phone on a short break, better to go for a walk or listen to the radio.

CHAPTER FOURTEEN

The Art of Memorizing

Good memory

There is a character named Shandon in the famous TV series "The big bang theory ". The guy can remember almost every little detail of his life since he stopped breastfeeding.

We have seen some of the famous people who can remember the value of pi up to 100,000 digits, people who can remember the phone number of more than 500 people in just 10 minutes and I am pretty sure you must have seen some stuff on the internet when you get shaken by the memorizing power of people. So, I am not going to waste your time by giving examples, let's move forward.

It's a wish of every student that he/she can possess a memory just like them.

Yeah! It would be great if you have this kind of memory but let me tell you one thing. In the last 30 years, none of the IAS, JEE, AIPMT, or any other national level entrance examination toppers was able to possess that kind of memory.

If there is no need for such memory for the topper, then I am sure that You also don't need it too.

Still, a good memory is required for good grades or for scoring a decent rank in any reputed exam. By good memory, I mean a memory that can help you memorize the required concepts thoroughly. So, if you are lacking in this area, ride along.

Few tricks to instantly boost your memory.

• If you think just by studying once you are going to remember everything, let me tell you one thing: you are living in some fantasy world because it's not going to happen. You have to revise on a regular basis. We will cover more about how to revise most efficiently.

• Don't cram without making a connection. Without connection, you are going to lose what you have read in less than 1 hour.

Let me give you an example. It is a powerful one.

I know it's going to sound like a joke, but I was in that stage where I could not remember my phone number even in 6 months and I tried this technique and within a day I was able to remember the 2-page diagram of engineering. Before unfolding this secret let me ask you something, suppose you planned to visit your relative in America from New Delhi. It's almost a 17 hours flight and most of the time the flight will be flying above the ocean. Just before the departure, you heard the voice of your pilot and to your surprise, he said "Hello everyone! I am your pilot for this flight. We will serve you some world-class food and drinks during the flight and also there is an in-flight spa. But there is a tiny problem. I am not sure if I can fly this plane. But don't worry; I have done it once or twice. I think I might be able to take you to America."

Now! Will you enjoy the world-class meal or spa? Let me guess, you will be the first one running out of that plane.

Our relationship with the mind is kind of the same. We are pilots of our bodies and minds. They are there to obey us. It is just we don't know how to make ourselves a master so they don't behave like slaves otherwise they are. And when we try to memorize formulas just 5 minutes before the exam, even though we already had revised the syllabus properly. By doing this we are giving our mind a very solid message "hey you, my MIND, right there, listen! you are no good. You are a stupid pilot "

Now you are the master of your mind. You might not know it, but your mind does obey you as master(if you are repetitive and convinced by yourself). So, it takes your message very seriously and starts acting in the very same manner.

Now will behave like a stupid pilot. And chances are there that your plane going to crash during the exam,

No trick, no food, no advice can boost your memory better than this.

Don't ever say to your mind that you are going to forget.

Give it all the positive vibes and assurance that it is one of the best machines. Just make your mind believe in itself. Talk to it. And most importantly, never get entangled in cramming because of fear of losing.

Say it to your mind that it can remember it in one time, believe it, and after a proper reading don't peek into your notes again and again just because you are afraid. When you ask your mind even after 80 years believe me you will remember it till that day too. Your mind will not forget during the exam. Just send this message to your mind and it will do the rest. **And the best way of sending this message is to show trust in it.**

Think this way, how would you behave if you had a CD or pen drive to upload all your notes and they would have allowed you to take them to the examination hall? Would you be nervous or afraid about forgetting something? If not, then why are you thinking so negatively when you have the best machine ever created in this universe. I know some of you still think that it is a joke, well it is not. Just try it once with all your will.

Believe me; this can change your life in a day.

CHAPTER FIFTEEN

The Art of Handling Tough Topics

One of the traps while memorizing is, that

"This is quite tough; I will memorize it in the next reading."

You know what, in the next reading you will have the same thought again, and honestly, if I tell you, this cycle will repeat again and again. Trust me, your time will pass just like snapping fingers and you will realize it when you will be sitting in the exam hall and your question paper is demanding you that particular formula which you considered as one of the toughest formulas and you will ask yourself, "Why the hell you did not memorize it in the first place, you loser!"

So, next time when you encounter such types of formulas or any tough concept. Just remember two things-:

Firstly, this is going to be your first and last chance you will ever get to remember it, in the next reading you will be revising it instead of cramming.

Secondly, break that formula or concept into small pieces, emphasizing the most confusing part. A concept or a formula as a whole is never tough so, there must be some lines or some parts which are making it hard to memorize.

So, you have to focus on those nasty parts. Try to stay there a little longer.

As they say in the army, **"More Sweat in Training, Less Blood in The War."**

The same is the case here, more time on confusing topics (better, confusing sub-topic or confusing line), less anxiety, and less confusion in the exam.

CHAPTER SIXTEEN

The art of Training your MIND to study

What comes to your mind when you think about a lemon

A juicy yellow sphere, isn't it?

Now think that you are crushing this lemon in between your teeth.

A little bit of saliva may also be secreted in your mouth.

You know for some people, just thinking of lemons can give them a sweet tooth experience. The reason behind this is that as soon as they think about lemon, their subconscious mind takes over the conscious mind and releases the same saliva composition which gives them sour teeth.

Our subconscious mind is a very complex and powerful machine. It rules over our conscious mind. It defines our habits and indirectly defines our destiny. But it lacks one thing, it cannot think on its own. But the good thing about it is that you can train it. You can make it strong; you can make it weak. That's up to you. You have to follow some very basic techniques and your subconscious mind will be trained accordingly. It's like a good trainable dog. But once you train it, it will follow its training very seriously. So, if you have trained it wrong, then chances are you're gonna get hurt rather than getting benefited by your own mind.

But sometimes we train it unknowingly, like when we sleep in the same room, same bed every day and almost at the same time every day. Our subconscious mind gets trained. Whenever it sees the same room, same bed at the same time, it triggers the sleep mechanism.

Most students study at random locations like on the bed, in the living room, or on the dining table. You might be there to study but your mind is not. It has watched enough TV in your living room. Now you are sitting there with your books but your mind is thinking about some TV or gossip because here it has spent hours doing that so all it thinks about is what it has done here most.

So you must train your mind for study. Choose a place where you will study and study only. It can be a study room, study table or a corner in your house. Once you sit there all you have to do is study. And if you have to eat, or make a call, read a message, have to take a break, have to listen to music, then always, and I am emphasizing here, always! you should just stand up and move 4-5 steps away from your study castle and do whatever you want to.

Never ever do anything except study at your study spot. It will give your mind a very direct and clear message that if you are sitting on your study spots it means you are there for study only. After 10-15 days you will see that your mind respects it way better than you do.

It will reduce your temptations and thought wandering to such an extent you never have imagined

CHAPTER SEVENTEEN

The art of Revision

There is no human brain that can remember something for eternity without proper revision.

I think every student should write this sentence and stick it to the wall in front of his toilet sheet so that, no matter what condition he is in, he should be able to read this golden line every day.

I would like to share a story with you. There were two brothers in a GURUKUL, Halu, and Talu. One day their master summoned them. Highly obliged, they went to the master. The master said that there are two very special rooms that have very spiritual power. So, it's Halu's and Talu's duty to keep these rooms super clean and they have been told that the master can visit anytime to see whether the room is clean or not by the prior notice of half an hour.

Both of them were very obedient, so they took soaps, brooms, and other cleaning weapons. The rooms were very messy and it took almost a whole day but finally, they cleaned their respective rooms. Talu was a bit enthusiastic and he cleaned the room way better than Halu.

The next day Talu was a bit relaxed as the room assigned to him was super shiny but Halu spent 10 to 15 min sweeping and mopping the room again.

The same thing happened the next day again, and the day after that as well.

After almost 3 months, one day, the master visited Halu and Talu. After giving the blessing he said he wanted to check the conditions of the rooms. So, as he mentioned earlier, he gave them 30 minutes of time. Halu again swept and mopped the room for 10 to 15 minutes. But when Talu opened the door of the room assigned to him. He just went into shock. It was a complete mess. There were spiders in the corners, sand was on the floor like a fine carpet and dust was on every inch of the room. He hurriedly went for the broom and mop but no matter how fast he cleaned the room he couldn't match up to Halu's cleanliness.

Now the question is, "who was better at cleaning?"

Well for just one day job, clearly it was Talu. But in the end, it was Halu who proved to be better than Talu.

The same is for revision. Some students study and practice a concept with complete clarity, and they get overconfident thinking that they already know the concept and the concept will always be there in their mind. But when they open the doors of their minds after 6 months or even after 1 month, they find that the concept which they claimed to be fully understood, is now gone. It's like they never studied the concept in the first place.

On the other hand, students who revise on a regular basis, find that everything is in its place where they wanted it to be. Even though they couldn't understand the concept fully when they study it the very first time.

You must spend at least 20% of your daily study time doing revision. And it will change the way you have been called in your circle, a topper or an average. You can

download short notes formats from our website www.thinkcepts.com

CHAPTER EIGHTEEN

The art of Practicing

Don't practice with a tennis ball.

Let's talk about Sachin Tendulkar, the great Indian cricketer, who scored 100 centuries in his international career.

Now when he was not an international player, he used to play for national trophies like the Ranji trophy and other equivalent tournaments. How would he have practiced? What do you think?

Let me give you some options

a) With a tennis ball?

b) In the nighttime at 2 A.M.

c) Only for half an hour

d) With a bat made of plastic

I must be joking, right! Why would a player who wants to be an international player do such a thing?

Yes, you are right. He never did these things. Thinking from a professional point of view he knew he was going to face a bowler who can throw a ball at 150 km/hour so he practiced for 155 km per hour. He knew that in the test match he will have to be there in the ground for almost 9 hours. So, while practicing, the time he spent was almost 10 hours on the ground. He practiced in almost every possible way which was equivalent to an international match.

I am not only talking about the practice routines of a sportsperson but almost every professional of some kind. Fighter, pilot, practice dogfighting on the simulator. Motivational speakers practice in empty halls. Even the tech-legend Steve jobs used to rehearse his presentations up to such an extent that his timing was almost errorless.

So, give me a single reason why you should not do it.

You know there will be exams and if you are preparing for any professional exam then most likely it's going to be conducted on Sunday. You will be there for almost 3 hours (depending on your exam). You know that day you will wake up a little bit early, wash up, and get ready. Then you will sit on a bench for 3 hours, you will be allowed to get up only for water or if you want to use the restroom only. You will see a complete paper set, without any answers.

Now give me the answers to these questions-:

Why don't you wake up early every Sunday?

Why don't you get ready like it's your exam that day?

Why don't you sit in your study spot for 3 hours straight?

Why don't you take a mock test paper every Sunday?

Why don't you use a simulator when every professional in the world is using it?

Well, you should. If you do it on a regular basis then on the exam day, your mind will not take it as a special day. It will assume that this is a normal Sunday just like other Sundays and BOOM!! You get that head start that you have wanted to have.

No anxiety, no fear, no stupid hormonal releases.

You will see that in the absence of these fears and anxieties how amazing your focus and memory can be.

CHAPTER NINETEEN

A little trick to increase your focus

Study while standing

We always study while sitting, so after some time our mind can get unfocused and it starts wondering.

Now if you really want to increase your productivity within minutes. You should study while you are standing.

It will get you out of your comfort zone and will increase your alertness.

The major disadvantage with this technique is that after some time you will get tired.

So, you better do it at alternative intervals for 10 to 15 min, like 15 minutes standing and then the next 15 minutes studying sitting.

CHAPTER TWENTY

The art of Question Solving

As I have the privilege to meet thousands of students who prepare for professional exams, I can say that this one is an incorrect study method which is found in almost 90% of students.

Whenever a student practices questions (especially multiple-choice questions) he/she checks the answer key just after solving every single question.

Look! When you read something for the very first time it's ok to read the solutions to questions. Until you haven't reached a certain level of that topic, it is OK to check whether you solved the question right or wrong. Initially, it will give you great insight into how you have solved it and how the author solved it. There will be some amazing concepts and short tricks that may change your way of thinking about that particular concept which is required in that question.

But when you reach an above-average level or say you have solved about 70-80 questions on that topic and now you are practicing just for getting mastery over that topic then change your methods.

Rather than checking questions one by one, just solve 10 to 15 questions at a time and check the answer key only after that. It's better to shuffle the numbering, I mean for example you can solve the questions which are numbered as the multiples for 3 like 3,6,9...like this, but do at least 10-15 questions at a time.

It will give your mind a little bit of insecurity about whether you are solving it properly or not. It will stretch your mind a little more. Slowly your mind will get accustomed to this insecurity and will learn new methods to cope with it and this will be a game-changer in the final exam.

CHAPTER TWENTY-ONE

The art of Rising

Again, let's talk about a very vicious trap. When an average or below average student wants to improve himself, he is either very motivated or very frustrated. In either way, his emotions are very high. He wants to achieve the tag of "SMART STUDENT "overnight. Though he/she already knows that this is not an overnight process but then, what will be the greatest of emotions if they can't kick your common sense out of your mind.

Look if you are an average or below-average student and you want to study like toppers then the first thing you have to do is stay practical and keep your ego 100 miles away from yourself. You can't solve top-class problems overnight. You have to give yourself a practical timeline. Usually, 3 months is enough time for a makeover.

But initially, when you study, start doing the easiest question first. After 10-15 questions you might think that it is just a waste of your time and then you will move to the next level but hey! Let me stop you right there and tell you to slow down; these questions are not for clearing your basic concept. There is something more.

Actually, this is a very powerful factor that can affect your mindset in the exam.

If you think carefully, have you ever been in a situation where you are writing your test and you are not able to solve a few questions (or more than a few). But when you see the question paper at home again after a few hours or days you find that the questions were actually not that hard. If you had pushed your mind just a little bit harder you would have been able to solve them during the exam.

So, what exactly happened here is that other than anxiety there was something else. You were not used to the language of the question. In the classroom, you have the privilege of presence of the teacher and at home, in your study room, you have the privilege of answers and solutions. Neither of them were there during the exam.

So, these simple and basic questions will make your mind get used to the language in which most of the questions can be asked. So, start with very simple questions and after solving 50-60 very basic questions you should move on to the next level. Otherwise, that concept will remain half ripened in your mind.

CHAPTER TWENTY-TWO

The art of Controlinng the Brain

Only fools celebrate before winning

In the circuses, do you know how were they able to control deadly lions and tigers?

Basically, there are two techniques.

Punishment and Reward. Their trainers give punishment when animals do not behave accordingly and give rewards when they do.

In the long run, the reward technique is more powerful than the other one.

As I already told you how our subconscious mind has the power to define our destiny and how by giving it proper training you can change your destiny. Also, we have discussed that it behaves like a very powerful animal.

Now the question is, How we can train this powerful animal?

Earlier, teachers and parents were very inclined to use punishment techniques as a learning tool. They used to apply all sorts of mental, emotional, and physical punishment as well. But we all know that this is not an optimum technique. You can make someone silent or make them behave according to a specific pattern for a time period by using this, but in the long run, it is more like a destructive technique than a constructive one.

So, what is a reward technique and how can we use it for our own benefit?

This technique exactly works like when someone does something according to our desire, we give him a reward. All the promotions in offices, prizes, and medals in sports are examples of reward techniques. Even money, which is one of the strongest forces that leads almost every person on this planet to do work is also a reward technique.People even do those kinds of work which they hate the most. If you do according to your boss's wish, company's wish, society's wish, market's wish you will get money as a reward and we all know that everyone in this world wants this reward.

We can apply this concept to our studies as well. All we have to do is give it a reward after completing the job. Like if your will is so poor that you can't read a single page, then make 20 lines reading your goal and give yourself a reward when you finish these 20 lines.

The question is "what kind of reward"? The answer is anything that makes you happy and which you can afford again and again. Candy can also do the job.

Now on the bigger stage, if you find yourself unable to study for 5 hours, then break it into 10 parts, give yourself a reward after each part and after completion of 5 hours make sure you kind of celebrate it with a little party. A movie with popcorn will do the job.

Please keep in mind that this is only for a few days, (excess sugar intake can be dangerous for you).

In the same manner, if you are used to listening to music, or movies or social media or gossip, (anything which can steal your time) use it as a reward. Just don't start your day with a reward, rather finish with it.

What you need to do is just finish your daily job, and then use any of your addictions as a reward. It will increase your productivity, also after a few successful days, you will be even able to overcome it, if you want to.

CHAPTER TWENTY-THREE

The art of following Timetable

One day, Raj attended a seminar and felt very motivated. He felt like it was just a matter of some days then he will be in the league of toppers. Not only class topper but also national topper.

But he knows that for this, he needs a plan and the first step he took for planning is having a perfect timetable so he made one as below.

5 am	Wake up	Usually, he wakes up at 9 AM
5:30am to 7:30am	Study Mathematics	
7:30am to 8:00am	Take a break	
8:00am to 10:30am	Study Chemistry	
10:30am-11am	Take a break	
11am-1:30pm	Study Physics	
1:30pm-2:00pm	Take a break	
2:00pm to 5:00pm	Tuition	
5:30pm to 6:30pm	Revision	
6:30pm to 9:30pm	Again study	
9:30pm to 10:00pm	Fun	
10pm to 5:30am	Sleep	

Quite impressive!!

Full proof plan. But the next day there was a teeny tiny problem.

He woke up at 8 AM!

And after that, he tries to study for 1-2 hours. He spends half of his day thinking that he is a loser, and another half he gathers all of his motivation that now he will follow the timetable from tomorrow.

The sad news is that out of 1000 students who make this type of timetable, 990 students fail it to accomplish on the very first day and then every single day after that. I said 990 because I want to give the benefit of the doubt to that 10 people.

So what went wrong!

In my opinion **everything**

Now let's take a different scenario. Raj is a very weak guy, physically. He went to a complete body makeover. By having the body as the great bodybuilder Arnold in his mind he joined a gym. He never did a single pushup in his life. So, on the first day how many pushups will be his practical goal?

5 or 50?

If he goes for 50 pushups then you know he won't be able to get up after completing 10 pushups (forcefully and painfully) he won't be able to even move his shoulder the next day.

The same kind of thing usually happens with timetables.

So, how should we identify the right timetable for us?

The answer is" by being 100% honest with yourself". As in the case of Raj, we already know his practical goal for the first day. We need that level of honesty here. If you can't read 2 lines in a single sitting, believe me, you can't study 10 hours the next day. Your practical goal should be to complete 2-3 pages in a day over the next week.

If you already can study 2-3 hours, you can push yourself to 4-5 hours.

The key is to push yourself every single day.

Initially, it is more important to follow the timetable without failing, than having a perfect timetable. Once you are able to follow it on a regular basis, you will notice that your willpower has been boosted to the next level and now you are ready to give a sitting of 3-4 hours with full concentration. Also, you will find your perfect timetable as well.

Some of the examples of perfect timetables for different types of students are:

1. Nervous King: the one who finds it difficult to sit just for 5 minutes

Your Goal should be: Page based (number of pages-based time table, not the number of hour's basis)

Precaution: if you are highly nervous and can't study for only 5 to 10 minutes, then don't set your daily goal to more than 2 pages. (For the first week)

Your worst enemy is guilt, as you are failing on a daily basis. So just think of yourself as a human, have sympathy with yourself (if you are feeling guilt).

Make a goal of 2 pages, and try to read only 2 lines at a time. Stop after 2 lines and then ask yourself "should I read the next two lines". After getting a yes from your inner being, proceed for the next 2 lines. Take a break after half a page if you need (even a long break).

Just remember only one thing, set your goal really achievable and then achieve it at any cost.

Increase your daily goal slowly and soon you will be spending focused and quality time with your books.

2. I like to Stare at books type: if you can sit for one or more than one hour but your output is nearly zero

Your Goal should be 3-4 pages per subject (per day), not more than 10-12 pages for the first week.

Say you have 4 subjects to study per day. So, you have around 12 pages. In the first slot, your goal should be to cover one subject (3 pages). Set a goal of half of the page in one sitting. Take a pen and put it on the line which you are reading. Move it along with your eyes.

Tip: slow your speed (around 50% of your daily speed)

After half a page, take a break of around 5- 10 minutes. (stay strict to it, I mean just take the break and you must return after 10 minutes)

After break don't go for the remaining half-page, first try to write the essence of what you had studied just before the break.

Take a long break after the completion of a single subject and then repeat the process.

Again, you can choose a smaller goal, but after choosing it stay committed

3. Hard-working but not efficient: you can sit for hours, can study seriously but your result doesn't reflect your efforts.

Goal: To solve around 90 questions per day (I am assuming that your theory part is good)

For reading, apply the same technique as the previous one (adjust your daily goal)

For questions: try to solve around 10-15 questions per sitting without checking the answer key. You should check the answer key only after solving those many questions (right or wrong doesn't matter).

After that, take a break of 10 minutes.

Repeat the process.

When you come back first check the answer key, write down where you did something wrong. Point out the exact error. Was it theoretical? Was it petty? Or was it some serious conceptual error? Keep the record and work on that very problem.

Again I am repeating myself. Initially, it is not about having the perfect timetable but following perfectly any timetable even a loose one.**You can download time table temphlets from our website www.thinkcepts.com for free.**

CHAPTER TWENTY-FOUR

Bathroom notes

When I was a student, my chemistry teacher taught me one of the best revision techniques. With the help of that technique, I was able to memorize most of the toughest formulas and concepts.

The technique is very simple.

"Make notes like a cheater".

Cheaters are very creative people. They are like James Bond (not exactly). They have very creative ways to keep them away from the examiner's eye also they have a lot of ways to hide a cheat sheet with them.

But there is one obstacle; this sheet must be very small otherwise to keep it hidden can be a very tough task. So what cheaters do is write things in small fonts, really small.

What my teacher told me is that I should make notes for tough formulas and concepts in the same style as that of cheaters. Then he said to keep that sheet in the bathroom so every morning when I clean my teeth, for those 2-3 minutes I can revise from that sheet.

I agreed and wrote almost 50% of organic chemistry on 3 pages and I started staring at them for 5 minutes every morning. After 3 months there was nothing that I couldn't remember in organic chemistry. Wasn't it amazing?

CHAPTER TWENTY-FIVE

Aptitude matters

I have seen students who were amazing in arts and other areas but because of parental pressure, they chose science. They were genius in many ways except science and they ended like a plane looser.

People say that you should follow your dream or do whatever you like. But there is a problem, in teenage when a student doesn't like his/her own hairstyle just after 1 year. Then how can someone expect that they will remain enthusiastic about a career which they just heard from some friend one year back.

It is plain stupidity.

Neither do they have any real-life experience about the career which they are going to choose (except some stories of a distant cousin) nor do they know their strength and weakness at that time? So a parent must consider these factors. However complete career counseling takes time and money both but a simple aptitude test can give you some useful insights about yourself. You can even take some free tests on our website: WWW. thinkcepts.com

CHAPTER TWENTY-SIX

Exercise and food

Well! Let's talk about a universally known topic. Everybody knows that healthy food and exercise are a way to an awesome life. The problem with this is that everybody agrees with this statement but yet most people ignore it. The main reason behind this mindset is very simple. Usually, after getting motivated some people start eating healthy food and exercising. Now if you have tried healthy food, you know that it's not as tasty as fast food and also if you tried exercising then you know that you can't be a bodybuilder in just a week.

Now for the next 20 -30 days, you will be like "oh there is no taste in this food ". Also, your body will be in pain; you might feel at your low in the morning. You will feel no motivation to continue your exercise. so these 20-30 days will feel like hell.

Now you feel tired, demotivated, with no taste for almost the next 30 days if you choose a healthy lifestyle. Believe me, it's like a century for most people, and worst of all is that you won't see any real progress in the first month.

The results that we are looking for are less anxiety, high focus, amazing concentration, amazing memory, and a cool personality. They will come for sure but after 30-45 days. And most of the people can't hang in there for that long and that's the reason why most of the people don't choose a healthy lifestyle.

It is true that many students can perform extraordinary without following a healthy lifestyle. But if you are on a journey from average to the topper, then a healthy lifestyle will give you an edge. Believe me.

There is no need to go to an over-expensive gym. Just a routine of 20-30 minutes jogging and some basic push up, skipping will do enough for that. Also, you don't need any dietician for a diet chart, just cut sugar, fast food, tea, coffee, soda, and cola from your diet.

you can download a free diet charts and exercise plans from our website www.thinkcepts.com.

CHAPTER TWENTY-SEVEN

Best wishes

I have huge respect for people who try to succeed even after thousands of little failures. Most people can't understand their effort and judge them just by their results. But in my opinion, they are the bravest souls who despite so much failure come to the battlefield of cruel world every day.

It is really a tough task.

So we have created a portal where students can get help.

A help in each and every aspect.

for example, whether you need ready-made timetable pamphlets to download or a personal coach which can guide you on daily basis or even if you feeling really low and need a counseling session you can visit www.thinkcepts.com.

Be Your Best Friend

Talk to yourself like a friend, a good and honest friend. Just be the right and best person for yourself first. Everything you do, you feel, makes you human. Sometimes you will fall, sometimes you will get lost. Just take one step forward at a time. It's not the world that needs you. It is you, who needs you with your right mind. No matter what your condition is, you can always walk one step, just take that and be consistent. That is all you need in life. The rest will be history. You will see, the day will come